T0142728

A NEW LIE

AND OTHER POEMS

A NEW LIE

AND OTHER POEMS

RAZINAT T. MOHAMMED

malthouse 𝒳𝒫

Malthouse Press Limited

Lagos, Benin, Ibadan, Jos,Port-Harcourt, Zaria

© Razinat T. Mohammed 2021
First published 2021
ISBN 978-978-58789-6-7

Published by

Malthouse Press Limited
43 Onitana Street, Off Stadium Hotel Road,
Surulere, Lagos, Lagos State
E-mail: malthouselagos@gmail.com
Facebook:@malthouselagos
Twitter:@malthouselagos
Istagram:@malthouselagos
Tel: 0802 600 3203

Distributors:
African Books Collective Ltd, Oxford, UK
Email: abc@africanbookscollective.com
Website: http://www.africanbookscollective.com

DEDICATION

For your radiance, Amma Kinini

FOREWORD

Do not cry like a woman, men often tell themselves in the face of difficult situation. What the heck do they know about bravery, enough to consign a woman to the catacombs of weakness, she who tore her flesh to bring forth the man! And especially when the woman is also an activist, an artist, that is to say, a writer. An encounter with such a woman is an encounter with the stark reality of the indolence of men and the dire diligence of women in the socio-economic dynamics of life and living. Razinat Talatu Mohammed personifies this diligence in her artistic activism as a writer and academic.

She's best known as a novelist of feminist realism which can be seen in her works such as *A Love Like a Woman's and other Stories* (2006), *Habiba* (2013), *The Travails of a First Wife* (2015) and her many short stories in books and journals. But with just one stroke of her pen on the genre of poetry, her artistic oomph does not only overshadow the brilliance of her prose but she has also overwhelmed her readers with the audacity of her poetic discourse. This collection of poems, *A New Lie and other Poems*, her first in the genre, has re-kindled the simmering embers of the clamour for paradigm shift in gender discourse in postcolonial African Literature. The poems demonstrate the imperative of reconfiguration of the ideas, images perceptions and idiosyncrasies that currently constitute a bulwark to women's fuller realization of their potentials.

The poems in this collection are sobering to the chauvinist, re-awakening to the docile, punitive to the iniquitous, and an elixir for the social malady of inferiorization, discrimination and insouciance facing the modern woman in Africa. It is from this angle that I see Razinat Talatu Mohammed as a significant voice in this era of new normal in society, and hence recommend the book for everyone as personal protective equipment against the vagaries of life consequent upon the pandemic.

Dr. Abubakar A. Othman
Department of English and Literary Studies
University of Maiduguri
Nigeria

OVERWHELMINGLY FEMALE

Razinat T. Mohammed

THE CAGED BIRD DOES NOT SING.............

Through the slits of the iron bars
I view a bird decked in elegant plumage
On her head like a crown, is her load
Too heavy for her fragile neck
Her claws, clutching tightly the
Iron bars for support
Against the windstorm raging
From all sides

At intervals her multi-coloured covering
Is blown open till her black skin shows
Its green, blue and red veins
Her beak, long and narrow
Closes tight on a worm for her young
Yet, through the sides of her
Lips, her voice rings out clearly

She sings some people reckon, but soon
They realize that the sounds she makes
Are clarion call to others--- they are
Sounds of agony from the pit of
Her belly to remind us of our
Ignored selves
So stand up, sisters, for
That caged bird does not sing---she cries!

YOUR OWN KIND

Mother, tell her that you
Can now see through the veils
That beclouded your eyes
And the generation of your kind
Tell her that, to bear another kind is
To nurse the other kind
And nursing the other close to
The heart is like bringing the
Dagger close to the heart

Tell her, mother, that she needs
Just one of her kind:
A young tendril to replace the
Old stem when it falls to rot
Tell her again and again, mother
That the mother maize backs only
The maize cob, her own kind.

THE PROMISE

Hold on to life, sister
For his cruelty cannot last for eternity
Be a stronghold to your kid
And let not the beast bewitch it
Till the land with the tips of your nails
And reap the grains with the weight of your body
Carry them on your bent back to the stall
And never look back under the tree for
You will get incensed by the sprawling rubbish.
Hold on to life by serving on
Bended knees the toil of your youth
When dusk comes, keep your drapes down
For the windstorms can blow the rubbish into
Your famished black mouth
Muted by prolonged hunger
Hold on but awhile sister for this hunger
Does not stop the heart from ticking
Just hold on to life, dear sister
For a tomorrow that holds the promise
To feed your mouths that hunger.

WIFEHOOD

Her roughen hands, her history
The uneven skirt, her shame
What pride has the blue sky
If its rays cannot relief or soothe your weather-beaten body
Or comfort your cracked feet?
What ease holds the earth when it cannot heal those swollen
    feet
Feet that plodded the puddle path of a generation
Where the rape of hope, of laughter and rest
Are a constant reproach?
Is this wifehood?
Do you call this motherhood?
When her children run the length and breath
Of the land not looking back?
To look back at the ashes that once burn brightly
The fire that heat the hearth and browned the *Kisre*
That filled their bellies?
What is the meaning of motherhood if all it does is sap?
What is the meaning of wifehood if all you do is toil from dawn
    to dusk?
Yet, the beast sees nothing from his mean mind set!

THE DANCE FOR LIFE

As a child I had watched in movies, all the crimes in Las
Vegas and
I had hidden my innocent face from the shame of raw flesh
Burning with desire for the touch of men's lustful hands.
I had thought that it had to be the end of the world
If what I saw were truly happening anywhere in the world!

As a teen, my prospects peaked as I blossomed in beauty
My only dream being to bag a University degree but
I was crudely told that degrees were fruits borne after many
    payments were made.
But I could not pay-- for my father was long dead
And mother was scratching the soil to feed her young
A responsibility that weighed on her frail frame.

I walked the streets in the hope of meeting a kind hearted
    soul.
A kind lady made me clean and wash for a pay
That at least I could save to earn a degree.
But the master's lust would not let me be
And I found myself again wandering in the dark, unfriendly
    streets
Counting the faces of passers-by who only looked and moved
    on.

As I walked I could feel the wanton eyes of lustful men,
Men whose kindness of a plate of rice came at a price
Men whose daughters were serenaded to sleep after a lavish
    dinner

But they must go out to lure others' daughters to lewd dance
In the neon lights in the hall of nudity of the 'aficionado's lair'

Should I dance nude for the old and lustful men
Who flourish in the enclave of lies and live double lives?
If these 'wise men' feel no shame in watching girls their
    daughter's age dilate their clitorises for their pleasure,
    should I bear the weight of our collective sins?
If these my father's mates, should watch wild- eyed and
    relishing my nudity
Should I wear a veil for their shame?
Should I cover my face when they pinch with sticky fingers my
    firm breasts?
 Whose shame will I then cover, mine or theirs?

I need a degree but what do these balding men want that is
    not in their homes?
Should I then not stiffen my neck, straighten my back
While dancing to *azonto* blaring full-throttle from the DJ's
    deck?
When these old men swing their bald heads in my direction
I know the sight of my glistening skin tickles an already
    impotent part of them.

Should fathers not teach their children right from wrong?
As I place my hand on flames knowing I am in a dance of
    shame at the 'Cave Club'
 I often wonder if I was born to eat the dirt under the feet of
    others
And yet, it is for me the dance for life.

THIS BODY IS FOREIGN

Is this me? This slackened heap of flesh
Collapsing midway like runny Cennasir?
Could this really be me, these venous arms
Shrunken like lifeless sticks?
What is this folding flesh around my once slender neck?
No, this body is foreign to me

What has happened to my gazelle-like legs?
Legs that have galloped the sandy paths of the city
From West End roundabout to Gwange 1 streets?
Are they these ones that break at the knobs?
These knobs numbed by paralytic fluids cannot be my knees.

My voluptuous backside that swung in rhythm with my
　　swagger
Now shrivelled to pulp, each lobe to its own device.
My thrusting and taunting breast that needed no bracing
Now nose-diving, flapping like a red flag heralding my
　　eventual defeat.
 My once voluminous lock of hair receding cowardly
From the temple, like frightened soldiers on a battle field.

These eyes that iced many fires like Bahiah's
No longer invoke Cupid's amorous arrow
To shoot into the hearts of my victims
To have them fully entrapped in my snares
But are these those same eyes,
These eyes that have turned the colour of ashes,

These squinting lacklustre eyes that see only through the
    rimmed lenses?
No! These eyes are not mine and this body is foreign to me.

What are these feeble feelings fiddling around my waist?
These feelings that bear no meaning and no pleasure,
Can I not at least hold on to the feelings and flow with
The rhythm of the Master Dancer?
But this heap of floppy flesh
This receding cavity of skull and withering scales
This apparition in the likeness of a woman
Cannot take my place--because this body is foreign to me.

WOMEN ARE FLOWERS

Lovers of flowers love women
Lovers of beautiful homes are lovers of women
Those who love their stomachs must love women
The tenderhearted love women for
Their delicate touch that soothes
Show a woman that you care
And have a world of flowers:
Your bathroom a scent of lavender
Your bedroom a chamber of roses and jasmine
Your bed a spread of lily and silk
Your pillow scented wool
To make your head reel into the white clouds of Nirvana.

WHAT WILL I SAY?

What will I say happened to me?
What will I tell this child forming inside of me?
How can the words form on these pallid lips
To tell the world the tangled tale of myself?
My heart carries a burden so heavy it can burst
My body a river of water and blood, mixed
And when I cry all I see is my tears?
Are some problems not deserving of bloody tears?

Ceaselessly, this child kicks and my heart irks
Perhaps he is furious that he lies in the wrong bed
Or desperate to come before his time
What could I do when the times have changed?
Strangeness takes over the land
A son kills his own father and ties the mother to her iron bed!
What do you call this phenomenon that has overwhelmed the
    land?
This son who poisoned his brothers for not toeing his line
What can I say about this harvest of woes?

Every woman has her own story to tell
My brick home, crumpled to dust, my hearth as cold as the
    dead
I am a woman who gladly suckled her infant
But must be gagged for a second suckle by an adult?
What then is there to tell except of
A woman's bleeding heart
Haunted by the twists in her fate?

If I could speak to this child
 I would speak to him about this world
That he would see its woes
And perhaps he would refuse to see the rising sun that soon
    must set
If I could wring his unformed neck
And pull out each artery with animosity
Will my desired solution come?
But ancient upbringing tells me 'life is life'
Its faint whispers fill me with qualms
What rights have I to take another's life?
Yet my humanity has been taken
Why should I live on, to feel these pangs continue to hit my
    fragile ribs?
Yet, my dying is linked to the dying of this child?
That faint whisper rumbles in my head like a bee buzz
'Even to your life, you have no rights what then of your
    unformed child?'
What life is this anyway?
When a woman is forced to lap up her own vomit?
When the snake sloughs its skin, does it return to wear it?
Is it proper for a father to view the nakedness of his grown
    daughter?
Or should a son pleasure himself in the nudity of his mother
    as she takes a bath?
These laws are not taught by words of the mouth but just
    trend…
Some rights and wrongs of humanity are not uttered yet are
    universal
Same in Pakistan, same in China, Czech and Yerwa

Tell me then how to pronounce my words to this child when
he comes!
Tell me what I will say to this child who is both a son and a
grandson!!

TALKING LOVE

EXECUTE ME

Before your shadow
I stand in court awaiting my turn
The turn of fate to deal with me
Yet I say, I want your face to be with me

You are the judge to weigh my sins and judge my case
But you judge my case not in court
You hide your face within our courtship

In the inner chambers or your heart
You judge my case and weigh my sins
"Condemned by hanging" your verdict
Says to end the case of my sins

And I fall to my knees and beg
The court to see your face
To see your face that I may go
To hell in peace

I wish to see the face of the judge
And ask of him just one thing; I beg the court
That he should be the one to pull the rope
That helps the knot to do its work

I hold so tight to the gallows' beam
And ask of him to see me die!

HEARTLESS

You took my heart under your wings
And flew away into the skies
You flew to earth and held so tight
The heart you took into the skies

I stood below and watched your
Wings fly above into the clouds
Taking with it my only hope
The hope to feel and hope to love

Now I stand below your wings
A frame for sure without a heart
It shed the light on why I
Hurt your heart so sharp and deep

For, you see, I have no heart to show
You love and have no heart to keep your heart
Thus, I hurt your heart for sure; you see
I have no heart to love your heart

NO OTHER LOVE

Since that day
When I lifted up my eyes and beheld your face
That well lit face that glittered with love
I knew that I could love no other

When you took my hand with that
Firm clasp, I felt the burning fire
 Melt down my veins and in return
I transfused the fevers of my heart
And the drippings of my eyes onto
That strong arm which led the way
Showing me the path that is my part

I have walked my life with unseeing
Eyes and men have passed in files like ants
Without causing a stir to the heart
But you came and restored life to a lifeless
Soul, sight to the
Blinded eyes and meaning to a
Meaningless life

How is it that I have lived for
So long without knowing about you?
And to think that you have been around
All the while only keeps me in awe
Of what might have been

If I had known such love
I would have done many things differently
Behold, your words say that "all things

Work together for good" and for this sake
I am able to go through life
Loving no other but you.

PURE MILK

So difficult it is to swallow that knowledge
Of solitude without that link that connects
The mother to its pre-natal child
Like an unwanted child, the orphan had
Been expelled from its symbiotic world
Into a desperate and painful lonesomeness

The natal touch had afforded
The rhythmic link where the infant mouth
Had been fed pure milk through the teat of a
Bottle so proudly guarded

And what is this hunger that it feels?
Yet will not want to be fed other milks
For a gaze through the faces of
Willing benefactors reveal the absence of
That dark face that fed the orphaned mouth

Like caring mothers, they have cuddled
To feed and the orphan had cried your
Name mutely as a tired child cries for its
Mother's warm touch and nurse

These goodly people had often recoiled
Back into their shells, thus withholding
Their milk of life
And the orphan had looked with those
Unseeing eyes into new faces as they paused and
Went without recognizing those same features
That distinguished you from all others

Famished will it remain until your safe return
To nurse your infant mouth

For who can explain the bond between mother
And child?
Or describe the taste of one's mother's milk?

MASTER DANCER

Slowly, the dancer takes his first steps to
The drumming beginning to reverberate
Through his heart—letting the warmth
Of his body feel the accompaniment
Of the music to which he must dance

With gradual ascendancy, the
Rhythm flows through his strong
Muscles, flexing them to the glitter
Of perspiration, smeared on bare chest

The music, playing a rustic tune,
Compels his body to coil, creep on
The belly until he stretches out in
Full length in a strong rhythmic
Body movement while his back up dancer,
Floating in the clouds thus, unable to imitate
His steps, gives up and only
Sways from left to right in a slow delicate
Motion with a degree of harmony with the
Master dancer.

The music becoming fiercer, stiffens the
Contours of the huge shoulders and
The face hardens with corrugated of lines
Which send signals to the back up who quickens
The swaying, acknowledging the ground
Tremor which ushers in the last steps of the
Dance and the prompt sound of the tenor heralding
The waking of yet another day.

THIS MONSTER

Like the bite of a little winged ant
That begins to radiate pain and swelling
To larger parts of the body, that little
Spark of care has graduated into
This consuming fire that is ravaging
An entire existence

Like that disproportionate creation of
Frankenstein's which turns around to
Consume its creator, that arrow which
Was shot to you
Is sworn to consume the life and
Fibre of an existence

The heart is void for it has been
Emptied of all other emotions 'cept the crave
The brain is fagged with messages that
Are only descriptions of a dark face
The arms are hanging loosely
They are weary from handling the
Imaginary you
And now, the face is purged of its
Glossy laughter
It hangs out from waste and grief
The entire body cries for a cure
What can you do, to redefine this Monster?

SO ARE YOU

When I look into your half-closed eyes
Deep down within those sensuous eyes
I see a glitter and I recall seeing same in the
Eyes of your kind that I call brothers

With them, I share that universal
Sparkle that blinds the eyes
Though we choose to keep ours wide open
Not allowing the veil of blindness to
Shroud the smiles that should soothe
The heart rather than smother it

In their embrace, I feel young again
For a young person needs protective arms
Not the arms where I catch the fevers
And the smooching sends me into the clouds
Until I become intoxicated and inert

Let me take your hand and feel its
Strength run through my arm so that I may
Feel rejuvenated in spirit for when he smothers my heart
I may have you to soothe it

So open up those eyes and allow
The crimson shines of the sun glow in them that
I may view myself anew through their sparkle and
Share with you that innocent laughter as I share with all.
For they are all my brothers and, nicely, I say
'So are you'

SAY SOMETHING

Your hands on my skin have grown cold
The heartbeat that I felt, lying there
Next to you, has now slowed
What is it my love?

Has your heart suffered an arrest?
Has it met with an accident at some delicate hands?
Is it determined to leave mine broken?
Does our fierce dancing count for nothing?
What is it?

Or has the inferno of another's heart
Consumed you that you can't see through the flames?
Has it scorched your tongue that you say nothing?
Oh! Say something…

MY TREASURE

You are a treasure kept for status
So do not falter because the
Treasured are never failed!
Treasures are forever!!
Stay hidden from prying eyes

My hands are still warm and
The heartbeat that you felt is still in tune
No! Nothing of the sort.
Let me hide you from those worms
So do not feel claustrophobic in your
Hiding place, for you will remain my Treasure
And I yours, hidden from prying eyes.

IMMUNITY

From hence my love, play the tune
And I will recollect my steps
In a dance of reunion with you
For in my heart is too much love
And its excess cures the heart of its affliction.
For the sick is often cured by an extra dose of the same
    sickness.
I will reminisce about my love
Not letting it crack the cage of my heart
Now I am immune to the beckoning of your love.

ILLUSION

A gentle puff sends whips of smoke into the air
Which carries you away from your beloved?
What cruelty lies in the hand of fate
That stretches out and plucks a tender heart
Beginning to feel the warmth of an embrace?

Lay still my love
That I may reach you in my trance
For I feel a gentle wind blow over my naked skin
Gently ascending with me into the sky
Bringing me into communion with you

The springy smoke forms your
Image so wholly that much gazing
Lulls both body and soul
Till the lips utter:
Ha! At last, the warmth of
That embrace is mine

UNWORTHY

So sweet are you
That, for a while, I pause in wonder
To ask if such sweetness is real!
Behold, in asking this, the heart has often
Been lulled by more care
This seems real only in the fact
That it touches on the reality

But again one wonders about a
Good mind ready to bend for
A little talk not worth a thing
No! It should not wilt
For the old flower still blossoms
In red petals and its
Fragrance can encompass the soul.

LIMBO

Wherever we are, whatever we do,
Our destinies hang over us like the sky above the world
With a fun-seeking arrogance you waded
 Into a life serene at last from fortunes
 But the destiny you knew not dragged you
Deeper than you expected into this
Serenity that was another's life

A view into a long standing commitment
Tortures your heart now trapped within
A serenity that ensures a fulfilled life
Trapped between the old and the new
The old is tradition the new your hope
But our traditions are our heritage

Yet our hopes linger on unfulfilled
Broken between the two, you stand loved by the old and the
    new
What secret longings do these two whisper in your heart?
The old you own, the new astray and foreign.

FALSEHOOD

A step taken in good faith
Turns out to be false
And to make it right
Another wrong move is made
Between you and me
Many false moves have we made
To cover up our shortcomings
The inadequacies of a relationship sealed in silver linings
Up in the sky and far from the reach
A unity of hearts, encrypted in cotton pads
Like the assurance of fire to cotton
We cannot see the light of day

TAO OF STEVE

You tickle and watch
Play with your tongue and wait
To see how the Tao of Steve works
On your poor victim

The eager heart craves
For another moment to feel
And hear your smooth tongue
Glide in the moisture of her heart
Little knowing that you learnt
And played the Tao of Steve's moves.

VENOMOUS

The coward sniffs around for ways out for
His heart is heavy laden yet the tongue
Is afraid to share the weight borne
For relief, he says words that only go around
The idea and further robe the coward in a snare
That is deadly until finally he gives up and dies
A thousand deaths

The heartless exposes the naivety in you and shows
You the world of possibilities at fingertips
No feat is impossible to him and the sky is his limit
He leads you up the mountaintop and promises to show
You the origin of the waterfall, giving you all to
Ensure a good trip, your hopes are peaked
Then he lets loose your belt at the last bend and zoom you
    drop from
The height to the bottom-- while he snarls at you from
The top and by his side, another who had lurked by
To make the climb with your support

The lover, mute to the end like a deadly serpent that
Salivates venom in his kiss that stills the heart

THIS ROSE STEM

Planted in the early morn
And watered by like minds
Its growth, a wonder to view
For, in days, it blossomed between thorns and spikes
That are long and mute

The petals, closely cropped, conceal
The craving of the luscious stigma for
The anther crowning the slender style
To lower its head for its pollens
There were no buzzing bees around to interfere
In a natural process

The style, blown by a soft wind, succumbs
And lowers its slender stalk with masochistic
Gaiety and soon, its deed done, destroys
The beauty of the rose, which begins to wither and fall

A wild growing rose should be nursed
Or pruned for its thorns can prematurely prick the unguarded
Then, the beauty of the rose will fade
And in its place, a painful stump which
Runs through the blood.

UNEXPLORED

The virgin lands have gone mute and numb
All their hopes lost
For the blind man's walking-stick
Cannot search beyond the frontiers

With an amazing gaiety the seer
Swings into the shrivelled dark interiors
Of the long unexplored fields
The dark patch that hides the soul of the hidden gems of the
Unexplored dark interiors

With a flood of tidal wave
The explorer seeks the unknown
Treasure of the land
Manoeuvring to his advantage the
Wealth of his newfound love

LET IT BE

Seeing you pine within
Drives the thoughts wild
For if you could, you would not
Chose to suffer so
But what can we do about things we cannot change?
Can we stop our mortal selves from
Acknowledging diverse and varied fancies?

Yet, beside you is a good heart
Look close enough
You will see it
For one is but the other
And the other's
Eyes still glitter
Illuminating the beauty beyond
Reminding us of the beauty of this existence
So, if you cannot shine it further
Try not to dim it.

THE MANGO IS SOUR

Wait! Wait!!
Do not taste that mango
For it is sour
Look close enough
Its yellowness is deceptive
Feel it, its hardness will assure you
That the mango is sour

The poacher forced it off its stalk
And lodged his deep claws into its hard flesh
Giving it the superficial yellow look
At its scar points
But the mango is unripe for
It needs warmth to ripen

Cuddle it close to your chest
Give it tender care; wrap it in the palms of your hands
And it will mature in due course
For you to have your fill
From the sweetness of its flesh
So do not eat of this fruit for
You are not a poacher to eat a sour mango

OF A PASSPORT PHOTOGRAPH

The meekness of a face clasped
To a head uniquely splendid
Reveals only demurely the darkness of the eyes
Which pierces the heart of the
Illusionist already devoured
By the wide, solid-shouldered sphinx.

LOVE: A HYPOCRITE

Love puts a veil over our eyes
That we cannot see the wrongs of our beloved
It casts a shroud over our conscience
That we see black as white
It places loads on our heads
Yet we fly about with ease
It ties our tongues
That our mouths cannot speak of our hurts
Or express our desires without feeling the pains of the other
Love is an invisible companion
That sees all and says nothing
Love is nothing but a hypocrite that
Hides its real self.

OUR TUNES

I lack the courage to search
I look around and I see just you
From sunrise to sunset we flocked
Dancing to our tunes
Tunes that we created to suit the heart

Carefree we had perched by watersides
And our laughter had whipped in the air
Ringing through the irrigated plains where
Farmers accustomed to the sight of you and me
Would take leave of their needy crops and greet us with their
    smiles.
Our love was transparent because we wanted it so.

Now our habitats are no longer welcoming
Because an alien spear has pierced your heart
Killing me a thousand times.
Like the coming of death, it did not announce its presence
It wrapped its cold hands around my heart
And took away all the happiness that I had stored for you
Leaving me with this hollow that knows only pains.

This prison in which you are is single-celled
It has no space for two
And I must stand outside watching you imprisoned
In a web not woven by my own device.

SO MUTE

Why so mute to the end?
What mercurial pebble weighed on your tongue?
The tongue that spelt out all the Nasheems
The tongue that spelt out a plan yet betrayed a heart
Was it so difficult that you kept mute to the end?
Was your heart not weeping for the innocence pricked?
The innocence of a desire so transparent you could see
    through?
Even in seeking forgiveness, you were mute on the real matter
Why keep so mute to the end?

VALEDICTION

You have it all
Little petite femme
All on the thirteenth day
Taken to the thirteenth house
By the dark-headed sphinx

The laughter is all yours to enjoy
And the lion's roar you will hear
The sleek surface will reveal
A thorny inside so be wise
To care and to bear

Nurse delicately with those little
Hands and the heart will remain yours
But relax a little and the sphinx
Will return to arms
Ready with tender care and soothing words

Beware for a dark-headed sphinx
Is the delight of many a lioness.

SWEET ENEMY

Tonight is yours to do as you please
Your prize is yours to keep as you wish
The chest yours to comb its tufts
With the strength of your little fingers
Those strong muscles are yours to
Rub against and feel their worth

So dream along sweet enemy
And drown yourself in the love
That belongs to others
And play good for it is by a breath's
Luck that you are not thread-bare

IN MY DREAM

In a dream you stood by me
In my dream you held my hand
And you said you will always be there
And you said I could fly to the skies
And still will find you there
Waiting!
Waiting!!
Waiting for me to come to you
To come and hold your hands
And my head was filled by the dream
Flying and seeing the clouds
The clouds that I see in my dreams
The clouds that I wanted to hold
Suddenly they had never been there
Suddenly they had melted away
Leaving me stranded, alone in
The loneliness of my dreams.

Leaving me standing
Standing all alone!
Standing all alone!!
In the loneliness of my dreams that I see in my head
In my head as I sleep away while the world moves along.

FOR ALL THE PLANS........
(For Florence)

For all the plans
That you sat and made
For all the dreams you played a part in
For all the laughter that you learnt
To cultivate for his pleasure

On that day, you held his hands
His eyes on yours, a soothing relief
And the heart fluttered at the count
Of the day-- yes for you had hungered
For long, one after the other, the count
Was as long as the waiting

And now—he's left without a trace
Where can you go to search for such a man?
Who will you ask about his whereabouts?
When you knelt in prayer,
Your knees gave way
Now you have to clutch to the crutches
And learn to stand on your feet
For it will take a while
For you to forget all the moments of laughter shared
It will take a while to learn the act of the first step
Even for the sake of a second meeting.

THE SETTING SUN

The sun is again setting
Soon the parting hour that tears us apart
Shall again draw us close
In faithful supplication

The Maghrib hour is dark
So you and I cannot be together
After sunset for opposite we are
Not bound by the laws of Him
Whose wish we must do

Look into my eyes for the sun is again
Moving to its resting place and
So must we, to our separate
Isolated places of abode to rest
Where I will pine for the look
On your face till another sunrise

THE PEST

All the troubles given you are but
Sweet troubles from a lover's heart
Like picking a rose flower and getting
Pricked by its thorns
True love is that love that shares
The bitterness of the other's heart
Like tempest, it boils and rises in
Both sweet and sour emotions
It ruffles those delicate feathers
Protected over a period of isolation
It settles deep within the heart
Devouring it layer by layer until
The heart yearns for nothing else
True love is this pest that I bear
This taunting that never goes!

A NEW LIE

The rest as you wish haunts the soul
The spirits cry within for freedom
The lying tongue is fatigued
It gets bitten by the teeth for deceit

The old woman's knowing eyes
Gaze in silence as they watch you
And me, fooling in our ignorance
They wonder about new ways that
Are forming in our minds
Minds that never want to give up
And wait for the due process

To create a new lie my love is
To create a phantom that will consume us
Without a trace.

SPHINX

All night I dream of love
As only you can give
All day I search your face
And find only my day-dreams

Illusions that shroud the heart
In a membrane delicately lodged
Around a heart that you wish to seize
Yet too rigid to bow

What arrogance fills your heart?
And deceives your ego so?
A man can be delicate and remain man
His words sending shrills of delight
Through a heart already subdued.

CRAZY MAD

These pallid lips whisper
No words since your departure
Everyone else thinks me mad
Though I think of myself as crazy
For crazy and mad may share a
Thin divide not seen by the sane
This paleness that is viewed is
Insanity from the heart for
I am crazy for you though
Not mad about you.

OF HUMANITY

CLINICALS

Sitting in this clinic
I see with amazement what
People carry beneath the eyes

First came a damsel
Draped in latest fashion cuts
Her shape nature's finest work
I stare to admire God's splendid creation,
I nodded my approval
To which my doctor returned a wink
Leading her into the examination room
Curious, I tiptoed to peep
God! I fell back to my seat
For what I saw was beyond my wits
Her thigh, a red patch of flesh
No! It cannot be, I thought
How did she manage to walk with aplomb?
Oh! God, these damsels are actresses

Next came a young man
Decked in flowing gown and gumption
My heart followed my eyes
But my feet held me back
As I watched the doctor dab his brows
To soak the shock just gone
Not taking in to appearances again
He let the man lead himself
Step by step, steadily.
Soon the layers of gowns came off like slough

Behold what my eyes saw from afar—
Yaws! Everywhere like tiny soldier ants

And like soldier ants they stung
For he scratched! Scratched!!
And scratched!!!
Dear God! It's enough for a day
For what people carry beneath the eyes
Is beyond my wits.

SODOM APPLE

My sweet Sodom
You delight in the act of
Standing alone on this desert land
Submissive to the test of the cardinals
What human hormone resides in your lean stem
That makes your milk so pure?
What strange metabolism goes on in that stem
That makes you both mother and child?
Need alone makes you essential
As he in the dark hut orders
For a white cock, a piece of white muslin,
Seven cowry shells and a
Full grown Sodom apple--all set next to the heel
Blend the ingredients which drive away
The dark one that goes into the weak
Give him here, he who is possessed.

A CIVIL SERVANT

A serving servant
Who is civil
 Yet cannot serve a peasant
Must be evil
See how he frowns
Yet sits with the crown
Never letting go
Though he screams the word "go"

WILFUL DAMAGE

A patriot you have to be
A popular national plea
Keep the nation clean
A task beyond the reach
Operation Feed the Nation
Brings a Green Revolution
Leading to war against indiscipline and corruption
Turns we again in corruption

A transferred chairman carts away
Household furnishing to a new abode
A minister's ballpoint easily and cleverly
Signs away the jack-pot and soon,
A wanton inferno
Settles the twitching brows
Of the public lingering in penury
And too quick to lose track
Congratulates the culprit:
Thank God, you came out alive and
The engineer beams with a smile.

"Our God is faithful" he says
In egoistic self-fulfilment
But, beware soul brothers, for
Wilful damage leads to woeful demand.

THIRD WORLD

"Third World" they term us
They who have beguiled us our greatness
What rights have they to call us so?
We scratch the earth with our nails
Gradually incinerating under the intense rays.
Our massive hearth lies fallow
While it's natural gem illuminates
Skyscrapers and opens sliding doors
Yet we cannot but slam our mouths
For fear of the trumpish burst
Of us as "shit hole"
We trace our histories
Linked to the cruelty of mankind
The cruelty that deprived the Blackman
 Of self worth and much more,
But how can we accept the testimonies of those
Who are the cause of our curse as a race?

ORPHAN

I am an Oasis surviving alone
In the desert of nothingness
I survive alone
I am a stranger in my land
For I know no one among my people
I have no one to hold on to
When blown by the blinding wind of life.

I am the deserted date palm of the desert
I stand the dastardly desert dust alone
And bear the sweltering weather
To produce the tasty fruits.

I am the orphan left to aloneness
Like the deserted palm tree
I may bear fruits whose seeds
Gentle winds will allow grow by my side
That I may not be left alone again.

LAYERHOOD

In my chick hood,
I was a queen
Nursed to health, my mistress tried
Coaxed on, I fed and grew
At intervals, came my viral milk
A sneeze from me
Sent them scampering
On their toes, stood my attendants and all
My mistress prayed and fasted
That I may live and grow

Specialist came in and out
Satisfied, they nodded and left
Then came my first great pain
With efforts, I ruffled and pushed
Tuk! fell my golden brown droplet
Hurrah! my mistress cried and jumped
Alarmed and shocked I watched her pick my pride
And soon I read the reason for all the care.

D. O. C.

I opened my eyes into this world
An orphan
I walked my first few steps
A slave
Chained by some invisible strings of
Exchange
I am cruelly handed over in a
Brown — Maria
I cried in my mobile — prison
And thought
Why should I be treated thus?
I, a newborn

MY FRIEND
(For Aduke Endeley)

A source of inspiration
That shines on everyone
An educator that trains the nation
A disciplinarian that lives by example
You are what others try to be
When loved, you are loved with a passion
Hatred of you has its passions
Never taken unawares
Always unassuming
When it's cold, you are cold
When it's hot, you're hot
When it's both you blow hot and cold
Never lukewarm, never lacklustre
Because you are what you are
That inspiration in our lives.

KALAKUTA REPUBLIC

Here I am on the street to Kalakuta Republic.
The street that overflows with people of all types and styles
Bandana on wrists here and there on the forehead in militia
    fashion
The air stagnant and thick smells only of sweat and smoke
For a visitor, its rancidity overwhelming but how could I wear
    a mask
And give myself away as a first comer?
So I inhaled the tangible air and thus, understood the
    meanings
Of the unending Lagosian hustle.

THE LIVING SHRINE

Is this the shrine?
This abandoned corner stone that hinges on life like *Abiku*
That spies on the world of watery images?
What prayers did you offer to the god of cannabis
That makes your shrine a cynosure
To people of all ages and followings?
Is it true that you were a prophet
Better known in death than in life?

You were the only eyes that saw the misfortune of your
    people.
You were the lonely voice summoning your brethren to a
    sacramentum
But deaf, dumb and blind, they did not bulge
To partake in your communion to safe your motherland.
And now the world mourns your departure
As though you have only just departed.
Fela you will live forever
In this living shrine within your republic.

A FATHER'S TALE

As you see me now
Wretched as I am
I had it all in my youth
Then, with maturity,
I afforded all
My aspirations not impaired
Yet you can see me now
Wretched as I am
My seeds I sowed
Wide and far
I leave assets only in them
My wealth is shared in their number
Each with his own inheritance--life
Keep them, I advice
It is my legacy
Use yours well.

I RETURNED

From afar, I saw the land
Lying bare for there were no inhibitions beside the rubbles
Can this be my homeland, my mother's homestead?
Where my cousins and I played hide and seek in youth?
Where is my father's marbled balcony?
The balcony where visitors squatted at his feet to seek
    counsel
Where is the Cedar table where, as a child, I had placed his
    morning tea?
I see a heap of rubble and wonder if that is my uncle's flat.
The beautiful French windows, an idea he brought from his
    travels
Overseas, lay scattered in splinters amidst the dusty desert
    sands.
The broken glasses of blue and green reflect the sun's face a
million times
Can this grey rubble be my father's homestead?
Even the neem tree that stood tall and proud at the entrance
Has a story to tell. Its trunk, deeply serrated, and the jagged
    edges
Speak of mutilation done in haste.
The neem tree is Yerwa's identity and could this sacred tree
Not be spared the horror that has befallen its people?
Where do I stand in the mist of all the ruins?
Where do I place my feet to feel the soothing touch of my
    motherland?
What am I to do when the hopes of the land are buried under
    the rubbles?

I have read stories and have watched horrors linked to my
   motherland
The origin of such horrors I cannot fathom
So I returned to demystify this wanton surge of anger
I returned to make meaning of the siege?

LEBANON

What is the mystery in the name Lebanon?
That at its mention a delightful thrill runs through the spine?
What are the secrets that you have hidden from the world?
That like, a shy maiden, you have hidden your face from the
    affairs of the world
Yet you have lived and played the rustic music of antiquity?

Flying over the Mediterranean Ocean by night, for me
The airstrip, like a thousand glowing tongues a welcoming
    delight provides
In the air the fragrance of frankincense and myrrh of the
    ancient
Narratives of the Arabian Peninsula release
To fill our lungs with unfolding memories of your beauty

My feet on your soil a childhood dream realized
For your name alone sends shivers through my body
Transmitting a feeling of déjà vu that is overwhelming and yet
    false
And like a jealous lover, I strive to overcome the strong desire
    to claim you as mine
When I know that the best I can do is commune with your
    wild blossoms scattered
Along deep gorges and steep hills, called Lebanon.

THE SAIL

Lebanon, the ancient city hewn from the rocks of ages
Sitting daintily above the valleys of the wonders of Jeita
    Grotto
And its therapeutic coolness soothing to the many stressed
    minds
Coming from a riotous routine in the need to live life in full
And to understand the significance of a redefined history of
    the world.

The boating along the deep interiors of your magnificence
Is a SAIL into the bowels of the earth's essence
For in your obscurity is the significance of the beginning of the
    universe
Hidden and prompting a reckoning of the wonders of your
    naturalness
That the world has misjudged you and, thus, is robbed of this
Natural flow of beauty that defines you.

Like pilgrims, we stand in awe of your alluring beauty.
This ancient city of stones and polished marbles
This fortress that shares in the history of the Silk Road
That meanders into the rivers of modern civilization

In the cluster of your people we see a convergence of the old
    and the new
Intertwined in the struggle for a hold
The old not wanting to give up and the new too insistent
So in your smallness, the two are merged like the Siamese

Not wanting to be set apart for they share a common
    heartbeat
One beating strongly, the other resonating loudly

Now it is easy to understand the connection that keeps your
embrace warm over our own WS
For, like you, he is able to sniff the many treasures and
    wonders
That are hidden in the deep of your bowels.
Like him, we have drunk of your sweet waters and eaten of
Your cuisines and will keep in memoriam
The crabby salads and the taste of pickles on our spicy
tongues

(Soyinka Foundation SAIL program: Study Abroad in Lebanon)

MY ARREST

What do I know of wars and curfews?
What do I know of the colours of the rainbow?
I am a maid used to washing and cleaning
To help a widow, and bring up my siblings.

Can my clothes not be old and torn?
Could I not walk in rags and get respect?
When the leaders operate an unfair system
Is it my fault that I don't have enough?

Do you beat a child and warn to be still?
Should I not cry when I am raped and robbed of my rights?
What do I know of wars and curfews?
Why do you arrest me for walking on the streets to work and
    earn?

I know not the colours of the rainbow
So why do you talk to me of wars and curfews?

A RESPONSE TO THE MARKAS POET
(The Three Musketeers, Ojaide, Balami and Othman)

What a sin that you three left for the Markas without the
   amazons
And with such animated delight your stories tell
Stories that neither bravery nor cowardice convey
For the missing amazons on your tails you avoid.
Do you now choose the sweetness of dates over a healthy
   cuisine?
Could you not think that the beauty of an Amazon was more
   uplifting a sight?
Yes! The Eiffel Tower, the Twin Towers of KL and the statue
   celebrating liberty are all edifying sights but would you
   choose to look at mere monuments over the contours of a
   waiting Amazon? What has become of you my son that
   you shoo these two to a site like Markas?
What is there to see in the Markas but the bitter history of
   mad men written in blood?
The bullet-riddled walls tell only a heinous tale and like the
   invaders' bullets on the ruins of the Castle of Byblos; they
   offer nothing but the memorials of whimsical actions of
   men
At a point in time in the history of man's evolution to
   civilization.
Do not mock our efforts with cravings for such a savage sight
For our hearts have bled during supplications for the safe
   return of our heroes gone
On a cruise for fresh air while the tables were being laid

Unknown to us, they had made a detour for adventure or
  curiosity
None worth the sacrifice and in comparison to the tender
  palms of the Amazon.
Do you accept to be witnesses to the wanton massacre of our
  innocent children?
Do you travel to see the infamous shrine where your people
  were slaughtered?

FREE THINGS

Your love is wrapped in my soul
Which you gave without a price tag
The best things in life they say are free
The air we breathe we get with ease
The next best things are very expensive
If man had his way, the poor would be eased off life
Water is not made by man and its bounties are seen in
The Nile, Limpopo, Zambezi or the Niger...
Since they are not manmade, that gives hope to the poor
For the poor have hope to fish and irrigate
Like air and water, you assure life

When in season, the rains come to bless
It rains over the houses of the rich and the poor
If man had his way, the poor would die of thirst
But, alas, the best things in life are free and the next best
Are expensive indulgences: big houses, customized cars and
    designer clothes,
Things we can do without!
What relationships do these luxuries have on our ages?
Born on the same date, sharing the same age, rich or poor,
Our day-to-day growth, a divine gift that knows no creed or
    heritage
In the end, no luxury can delay the inevitable end, rich or
    poor.

LUXURY

Does having a big house filled with stainless steel wares
Or having a fleet of signature automobiles and the latest
   iPhone
Mean that one is living in luxury?
What is the meaning of the term luxury to you?
Does eating a bowl of Pounded Yam with *Egusi* soup sporting
   meat from chicken, goat, grass-cutter in addition to *Shaki,*
   Roundabout, Pomo, Stockfish, Smoked Fish, and Snails
   mean living in luxury?
Or does having a swollen bank balance and rows of wardrobe
   mean luxury?
What is the meaning of this term to a man of means?

Neither the velvety body wash nor the silk night gown can
   create the feeling of luxury
Without the willing suspension of belief in reality
Luxury is that particular instance when you are suddenly
   sucked in space
When you cannot seek yourself because you are lost in time
Moments that you cannot, with certainty, say where you have
   been
Or adequately relate your missing self in time and space to
   another.

Do the cars you drive give you that levitation-moment when
   you float in oblivion?
Between being alive and being dead?
Can you point a finger at the spot where you feel the smooth
   sheet combat your naked skin?

Can you tell, Oh! Can you just tell the exact point that it
     bathes your soul
Like you would an unfortunate fish at the roaster's pond?
Luxury is in the feeling and not the material
It is an intangible numbness that swirls the mind and causes
     one to be lost to the world.
It is that moment when, from a window view, you behold the
     Grand Canyon
And knowing that you have no words to explain the
     phenomenon, before your eyes,
You surrender to the willing suspension of reality and wonder
     whether you are dead or still alive.

THE GLOBAL SNEEZE

Often I have been told that life is a leveller
Never did I realize till I witnessed the world come to a
    standstill
Is it the effect of living in a global village that makes a Bat-
    eating Chinese
Sneeze and someone in Nigeria catches the flu?
What do I know of airplanes or cruise ships that take
    adventurous people to other lands?
What do I understand from the habits of eating wild cats and
    cockroaches?
How is it my concern that Li Cheng loves these strange
    habits?
Except that the big gangs have again gone globetrotting and
    have partaken
In the juices of the white bats and green vultures of China
Now, I am forced to stay at home with nothing to calm the
'many worms'
Ever increasing in the pit of my belly.
I was told that the season of sneezes is at hand and that the
    big and mighty
Are the first culprits. I shuddered to learn that like me they
    have to stay at home
But unlike me, they have no gnawing worms in their bowels.
But if they have to stay at home, frightened like me, then
    something grievous has hit the World for it is not normal
    for the big gangs to stay in self-isolation.
Worse of all, to remain in poor Nigeria and not be flown out in
    air ambulances

To other countries where leaders have put their consciences
    to the test
And have ensured that facilities work for their own benefits.
Our gang of bandits would, shamefacedly, crash in on
    meagre facilities of the masses.
But that is not even available in this scenario because the
    Coro is God's hand that levels
The big and mighty bandits to the rump of those on the
    ground.

MISERY

A brief presence it was my love
Your dark face still has its hold
On the strings of my heart
My veins boil to overflowing
To constantly know you are
Gone with the wind
What shall I do to reach you?
When all I see is your shadow
Too many times I feel your
Presence in the bathroom,
Your hand longing to scrub my back
Even as I feel that you are whispering
Into my ears, to warn that the water has not washed
The middle part of my back or
How the lather lurks in the groves of my waist

In the kitchen you instruct on what I must eat
When I retire at night, I lay still on my bed
Eyes closed that I may recreate your face and crave your love
Alas! My arms are spread in a void
Show your face tonight, my love, and
Let me stare into your eyes
Before you descend into the abyss
That darkness that consumed you without a trace
Let your face linger awhile
That I may read the engraved message
And, perhaps, reach an understanding of why you had to
    depart.

YOUR LOAD ON MY HEAD

I will carry the load on my head
If that will be enough to keep you by my side
My head-tie a crown for a clown
How could I fail to see the love in your eyes?
Unknown to me, it bore holes in my heart
I neither felt the heat nor the pain but
When my mother broke the news to me, I believed her only
    because
She was my mother.
My eyes are weary from tears that are refusing to dry
How can I go on when you left still thinking I
Sat on the pedestal and acted as a queen
When all I needed was to hear you say you cared
How could I understand your silent voice when it spoke no
    clear tongue?
And yet, my heart weeps for no one but you
And I will carry this burden on my head for it is
Your load and I am doomed to carry it to the grave.

WHY LET HER GO

You were lovers as your glittering eyes revealed
In your company then, your smiles radiating the fullness of
    your hearts
Admired by your friends and foes
Bile seeking and star-crossed souls, is that your new identity?
Think about the memories created in the country home
The babies made all in your name
What can a woman give to a man more surpassing?
She is frail but you are strong
Why let her go for simply telling you her needs?
Can a child fail to cry when beaten?
Can the hungry child not even ask for a piece of bread?

SHE NEVER WAS INTO YOU

In her eyes, I saw the glittering world
I was cautious but waited because I knew time would tell
Her many needs an extra effort to meet
I watched as you drove yourself the extra mile
But what was I to do when you could not see where I stood or
Even notice the fierce fire burning in my heart.
You ran like a panther into the coiling grip of the python
A beautiful snake that lashes out its slitting tongue
That tongue that dampens your soul with its cold saliva laden
   with death
And you, thinking it was meant to be, slid into the treacherous
   bosom of
A viper in the image of a damsel.

THE HIGH CAN ALSO FALL

When the news was broken
Of the ultimate fall of the head of the big gang
Tongue in cheek, the nation watched as his friends
Scared to touch his remains stood at a distance
In morbid resignation, they hid their expressions behind
    masks
As they all have always masked the affairs of the nation
Could this be the day of reckoning?
A day when members of the big gang realize
That the routes to their recreation and medicals abroad have
    been abruptly
Locked down in their faces, not by the opposition party but by
    the invisible organism,
The Coronavirus scare of the moment has subdued their
    boisterous show offish-ness
And the common man on the street shrugs off the presence
    of the virus
That is avoided by precautious hand-washing and distancing
    because they
Know that they have a greater virus to contend with
The virus that no amount of hand-washing can clear
The virus that no length of distancing can prevail on
The virus of having nothing to live on is worse than the
    pandemic
And given the choice, they would have the virus of washing
    their hands
So they can put some morsels into their famished mouths.

I AM A HEROINE
(Surviving another ASUU Strike)

I must pat myself on the shoulder
For I have survived yet another battle against the Federal
  Government
How did my brothers and sisters survive the worst neglect in
  the history of our struggles?
My monthly stipends seized by vultures whose claws are
  sharp and deadly,
The lockdown, another battle for survival
Determined to compel my roving legs from other beneficial
  engagements

I am a heroine because I refused to lend my hand to the
  wanton IPPIS
That has deceived the weak into hurried submission like a
  man who scoops upon
His head, the earth from a grave that is not his.
Do you pour the soft brown earth on your own head and bury
  yourself while still alive?

I am a heroine because I withstood the hard-hearted
accountant who thinking
His own way, pushed me to the end of my tether.
I will clap for you my brothers and sisters for not succumbing
  to the temptation
Where your colleagues smiling to the bank would flash mint
  notes to your withered faces;

I will clap for you for not throwing in the wet towels in spite of
the reddened carrots in the hands of others who, thinking
only of the present, would sell their birth rights.
I will clap for you all because you are the heroes of our time
I will clap for you because you have fought two giants with
nothing in your hands
In your empty-handedness, you renounced the monster
scheme that covers its face
With a dark veil
In your empty-handedness, you fought the centenary virus
that swooped over the
World in the night and, by the morning, a new order is born.
You faced both adversaries
With astute confidence that only being born strong can
explain.
I salute you my brothers and sisters for not forsaking the
struggle in spite of
All the difficulties that you had to endure.
Thank you my brothers and sisters for stoically holding brief
for the future of our children
Who knowing nothing would play the blame game with you.
Thank you all for giving me cause to believe that I too can
withstand the tentacle of the
Dragon-headed system.
Aluta Continua, a vitoria e certa

THE NEW WORLD

It is a new world, yet it mirrors the old
Is it not strange that the history of slavery, of which Mr
    Adelusi
Spoke so venomously of has never really ended?
The abolition of slave selling and ownership they said was in
    1807
By a mere proclamation by King George's feather-pen
And when those big iron bars were lifted half way above the
    heads of those bended Negroes
Who, too weary to see, believed they were free for life.

Today, three hundred years later, your children are subjected
    to civilized humiliation
Today, three hundred years on, your bloodline is hunted in
    cinema halls that show
Advancement in 3D goggles, a new world is possible they cry
But how new is this world to your offspring?
Does the old mirror of medieval past, exhumed from
    archaeological ruins,
Reflect what is placed before it?
Or does it reflect an imprinted image carved on it by the
    hands of the slave drivers?
Are they chips from old blocks or moulds of the old folks?
Are they copies like Angelo's celebrated Mona Lisa whose
Replica identities are scattered around the world?

Tell the world that nothing has changed
The hood-wearers have replaced the wig-wearing masters

Should the world not slow from its race against itself to
    ponder on the maggots
That outlived the corpses of the slave owners?
What is this choking that I feel around my neck?
What weight do they place on your neck that is heavier than
    the rusty chains of Elmina?
Discarded along the narrow alley from whence your
    ancestors
Dragged on the voyage to the new lands of Georgia along the
    Atlantic?
What new device have you contrived that you trap both his
    hands in cuffs?
What is this airlessness that is snuffing the life out of him?
Do you not understand the tongue that he speaks?
Or are you so blinded by your false strength that you snorkel
    the life out of him
Even when he cries, "I CAN'T BREATHE!"?

Printed in the United States
by Baker & Taylor Publisher Services